DOUG THE PUG

The KING of POP CULTURE

Leslie Mosier

St. Martin's Griffin
New York

DOUG THE PUG. Text and photographs copyright © 2016 by Leslie Mosier.
All rights reserved. Printed in China. For information, address St. Martin's
Press, 175 Fifth Avenue, New York, N.Y. 10010.

www.stmartins.com

Designed by Susan Walsh

The Library of Congress Cataloging-in-Publication Data is available upon
request.

ISBN 978-1-250-10082-5 (paper over board)
ISBN 978-1-250-10582-0 (e-book)

Our books may be purchased in bulk for promotional, educational, or
business use. Please contact your local bookseller or the Macmillan
Corporate and Premium Sales Department at 1-800-221-7945, extension
5442, or by e-mail at MacmillanSpecialMarkets@macmillan.com.

First Edition: November 2016

10 9 8 7 6 5 4 3 2 1

To my parents. Thank you for cultivating my creativity, giving me my first camera, and supporting me on whatever crazy endeavor I chose to take on. I love you.

ACKNOWLEDGMENTS

To everyone at St. Martin's and Macmillan, especially Daniela and Lauren, thank you for making a dream of mine come true by being my partners in this crazy journey. I knew from the moment Doug started running laps around the Flatiron building and everyone just smiled and took photos that I had found my literary home.

Jamie Coleman and everyone at Boxtree, thank you for publishing me in the UK, which has always been a dream. I can't wait to visit with Doug.

Melissa, I knew you were a match made in literary-agent heaven from our first awkward and hilarious phone call. Thank you for being my biggest champion and always pushing me to be greater. You never fail to make me laugh and realize the bigger picture. Now that this book is out, we need to have a celebratory drink—or three.

Tori . . . oh, Agent Tori. The first person to ever call me and say, "Let me help you." Look where we are now! I can't thank you enough for allowing me to text you like a crazy person at all hours of the day and for getting ramen with us in NYC after a long day of shooting, when I could hardly talk because I was so tired. We've come such a long way, and I owe so much to you.

To Brian Koerber and the whole team at Mashable, the first people to ever take a chance on my little Dougie and introduce him to a worldwide audience; "Thank you" doesn't feel sufficient.

Hadley, thank you for coming onto the Doug team and adding so much joy. You go above and beyond, and we are so thankful for you!

Andrew Cook, you're one of the coolest and most connected and loved people I know, and somehow you don't even know it. Thank you for always brainstorming with me and believing in where this could go.

Lauren Robinson, without you I would be so, so lost in the crazy world of money and taxes.

Mindy, Robert, Cheeky, and of course Mrs. Sizzle—my OG New York City crew—thank you for always ensuring that Doug was the best-dressed dog on the block. Because of you guys, he's officially the World's Best-Dressed Dog! Who could've known that our first photo shoot in Nashville would lead to such an incredible and lasting friendship.

Aimee, Carla, Peg—my Nashville pug squad—you guys have been nothing but insanely supportive from the start. I can't wait to have mimosas with you at the next pug party.

Josh Terry, you are a major reason why I am here today. Thank you for being my mentor and teaching me all I needed to know to do this on my own. I couldn't have asked for a better first boss.

Laura, Mike, and Adam at Gersh, thank you for being an amazing team to work with, and, Laura, thank you for being one of the most enthusiastic Doug fans I know (surprise, you get a free calendar this year).

Mom, Dad, and Danny, you're the best and most supportive family I could have ever asked for. You guys are my biggest fans and even though you may have been skeptical when I first told you I was quitting my job to become a dog momager, I am so insanely thankful for all that you've done for me throughout my entire life. Mom, thank you for being Doug's biggest fan (@dougsgrandma on Instagram . . . follow her, it's amazing) and my best friend in the entire world. I love you, Madre. Dad, thank you for helping me on every school project, taking me to piano lessons and concerts, and showing me that weird is cool. Danny, thank you for being the best big brother I could have asked for. I can't wait for your book to come out one day.

To my amazing family—Nana, Auntie Shark, Auntie Kathy, Grandma, and everyone else—thank you for loving me unconditionally and supporting me no matter what I do. I love and miss you guys so much.

Rob, my everything, there is no one else I'd rather share this crazy journey with. From early-morning flights and long layovers to photo shoots that last all day, you are without a doubt the reason why we've made it this far. I've never met anyone like you, and you are a light to everyone you meet. With that, your entire (gigantic) family also deserves an incredible thank-you: You guys are a crazy bunch, but a crazy-supportive and loving bunch. Thank you for inviting me into your family. I love you.

Doug's fans—wow. Thank you for turning my little Instagram account into something amazing and wonderful and for allowing me to pursue my dreams. Thank you for coming to the meet and greets, for your sweet e-mails, and for stopping us on the street to get a selfie with Doug. Without you, none of this would be possible.

All of my amazing friends, thank you for supporting me, cheering me on, and helping me choose between caption A or caption B for a photo. I love you all.

Doug the Pug, I know you can't read this, but since you're practically like a little human, I had to say thank you. Thank you for bringing so much happiness to people around the world. Thank you for teaching me about life and not even knowing it. We have a long journey ahead, bubs.

Of course my hair looks perfect right before I get in the shower.

Surfin' pug

I'm with the band, backstage pass and all.

I can show you the world.

Straight-up Pug Life

ALL
DRESSED
UP

Who wants to cuddle and watch Harry Pugger movies all day?

Breaking Pug

The cold never bothered me anyway (said no one, ever).

FOOD:
MY REASON
FOR LIVING

Brunch the morning after the Christmas party

HAVE YOURSELF
A PUGGY LITTLE CHRISTMAS
(AND OTHER HOLIDAY FUN)

I shouldn't have been left in charge of the turkey.

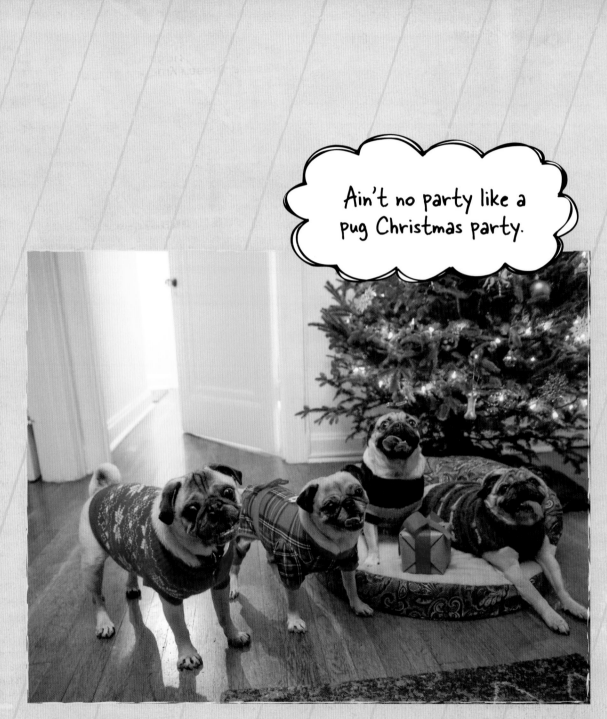

In loving memory of Nushi

A Pugmas Story

HANGING
WITH MY CREW

Jane Lynch and Matthew Morrison, will you watch Glee Christmas episodes with me?

Good luck saying no to this face.